## A CUT AND PASTE ACTIVITY BOOK FOR KIDS

### Food Edition

♥ THANK YOU SO MUCH FOR YOUR PURCHASE!

IF YOU ENJOYED THIS BOOK, PLEASE CONSIDER LEAVING A REVIEW ON AMAZON.

YOU CAN ALSO FIND MORE COOL BOOKS BY SCANNING THE CODE BELOW!

please practice scissor safety while creating your masterpieces!

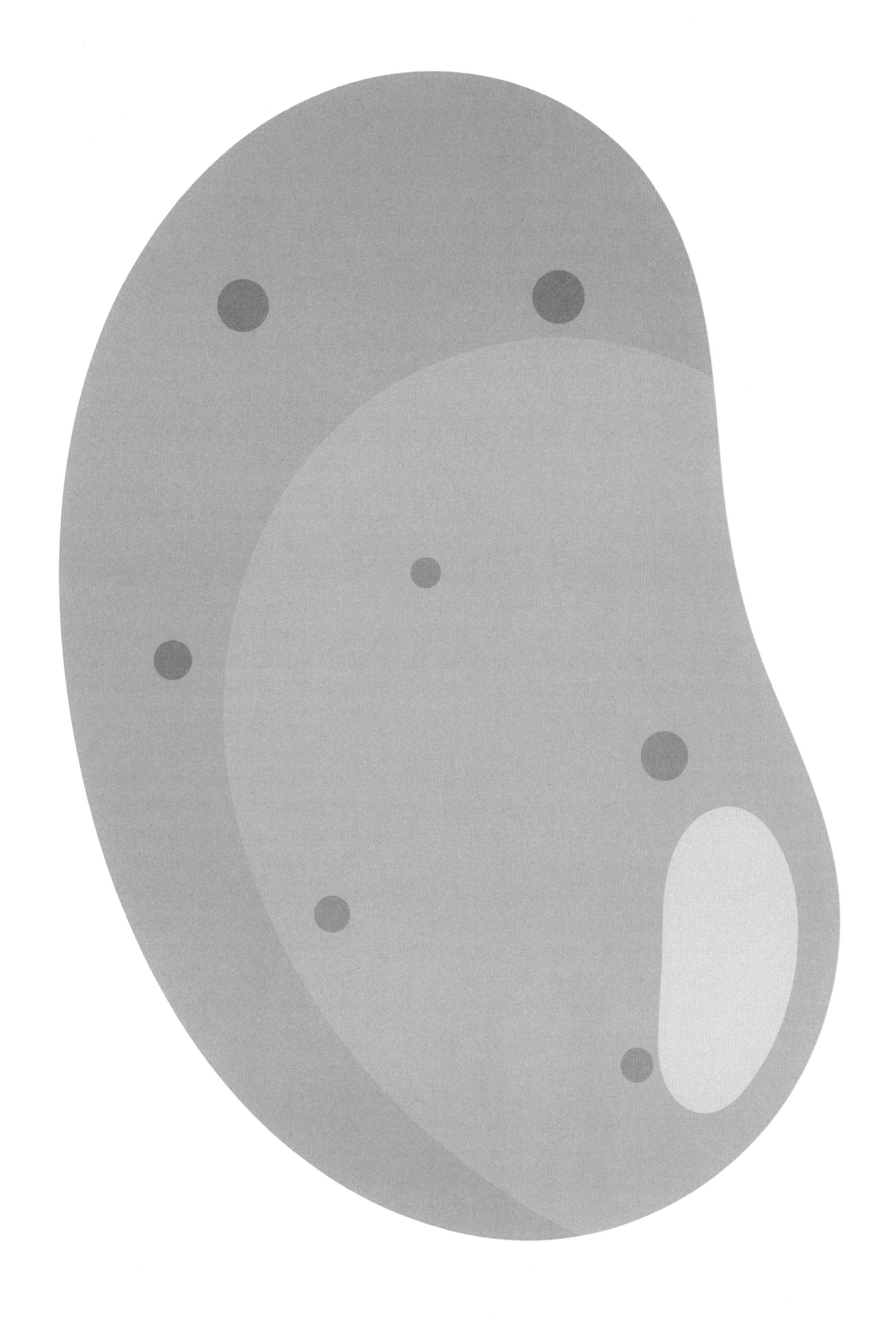

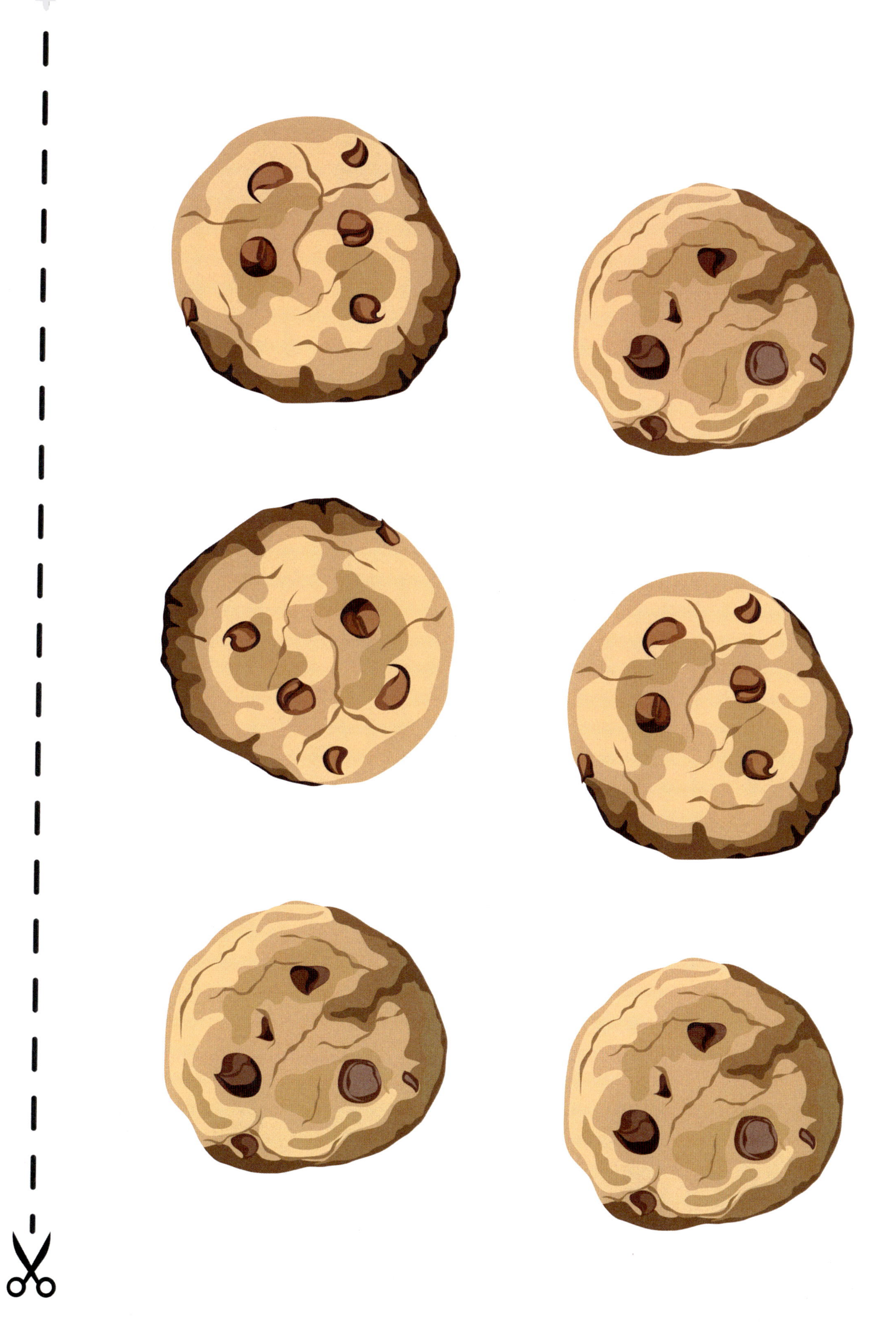

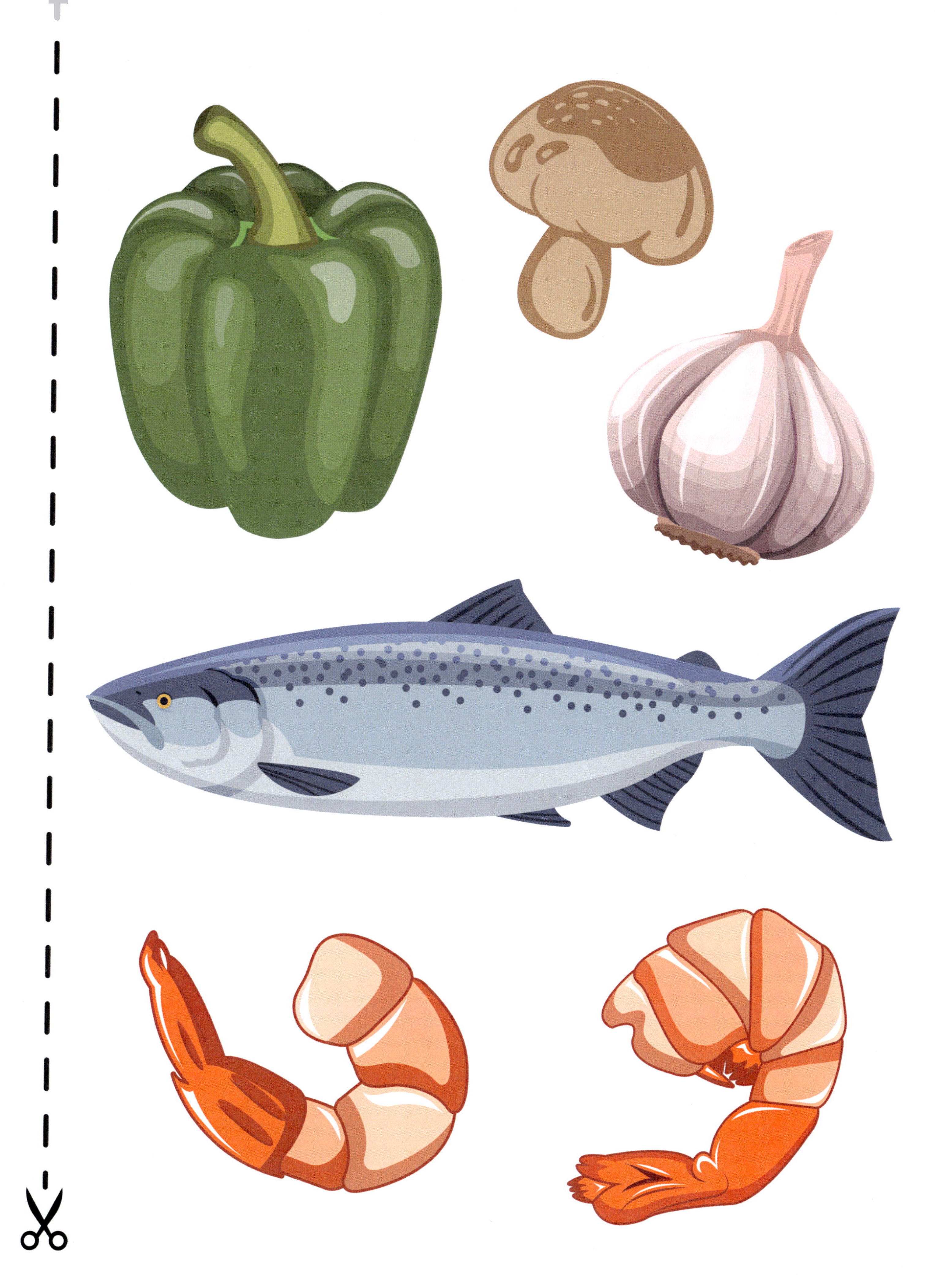

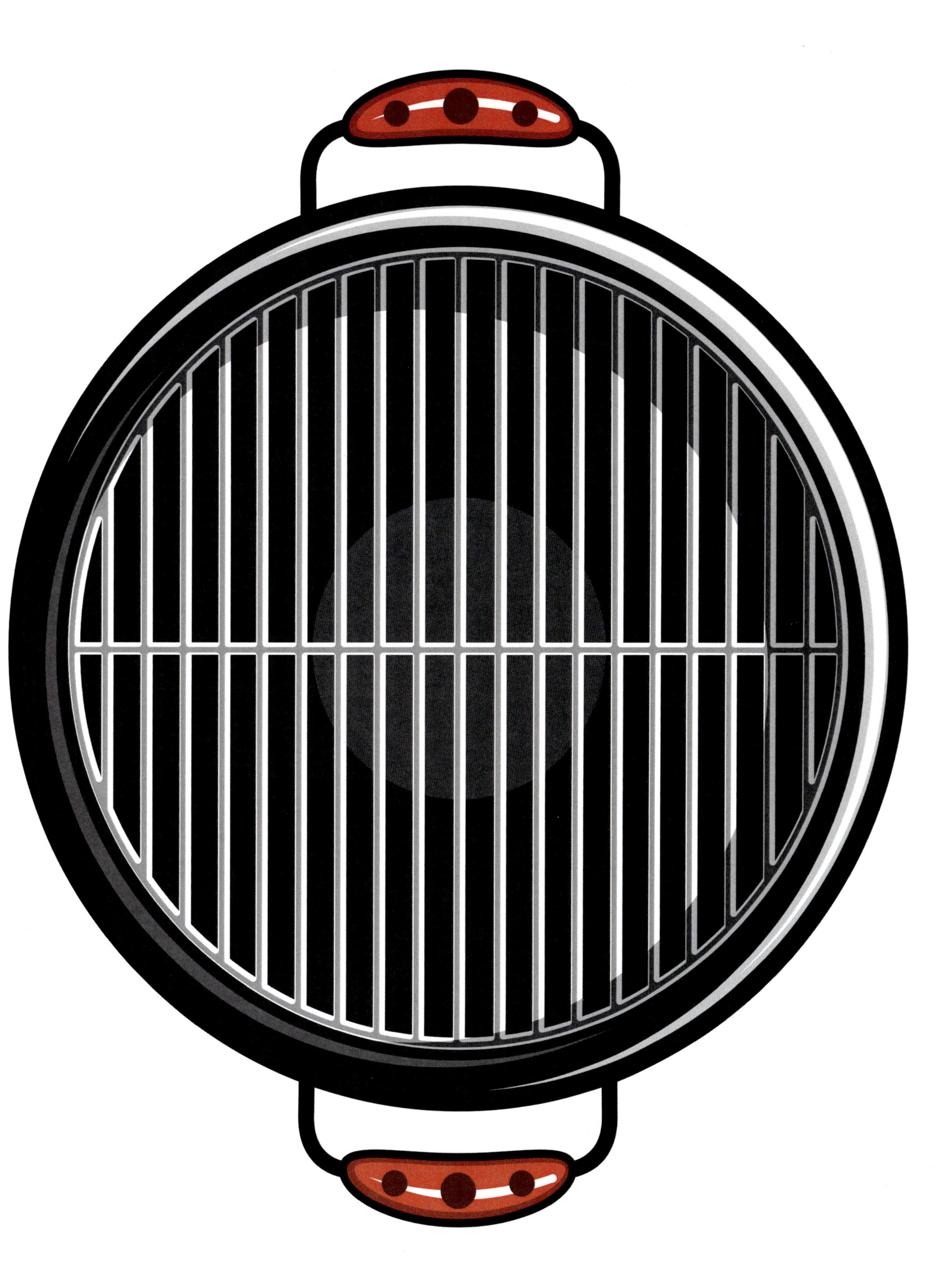

DREAMYNIGHTPRESS.COM/FREECOLORINGPAGES

Made in the USA
Monee, IL
28 July 2025